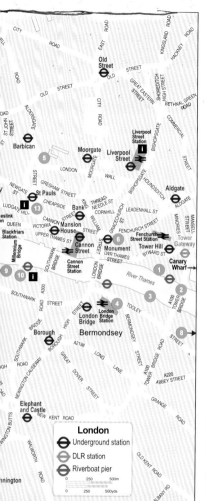

MAP KEY

1 Tower of London
2 Tower Bridge
3 HMS *Belfast*
4 London Dungeon
5 Museum of London
6 The Monument
7 Somerset House
8 Greenwich
9 Tate Modern
10 Shakespeare's Globe
11 Imperial War Museum
12 London Eye and the South Bank
13 St Paul's Cathedral
14 Trafalgar Square
15 National Gallery
16 National Portrait Gallery
17 Horse Guards
18 Downing Street
19 Cabinet War Rooms
20 Houses of Parliament
21 Buckingham Palace and The Queen's Gallery
22 Royal Mews
23 Changing of the Guard
24 Westminster Abbey
25 Westminster Cathedral
26 Tate Britain
27 Piccadilly Circus
28 Sherlock Holmes Museum
29 Covent Garden
30 London Transport Museum
31 British Museum
32 Madame Tussauds
33 The Royal Parks
34 London Zoo
35 Harrods
36 Science Museum
37 Natural History Museum
38 Victoria and Albert Museum
39 Kensington Palace
40 Notting Hill

THE ROMANS & THE ANGLO-SAXONS

43–1066

In AD 43 Roman legions, under the leadership of Emperor Claudius, came north to Britannia. The site chosen for their new provincial capital, a place to settle and establish supply routes to the Continent, was a great tidal river, deep enough for ships but not too wide to be bridged – the River Thames. Celtic people could have already settled here earlier to live and trade. So Roman Londinium became the crossing point and the first London Bridge was built in around AD 50, while new roads stretched south, west and north. The settlement grew rapidly.

Statue of Boudicca

The new Roman city suffered a disaster within ten years of this bridge being built. The Iceni tribe, led by their queen Boudicca, rose in revolt. Boudicca's army sacked first Colchester and then London, burning the new buildings and slaughtering those citizens who had not fled. After Boudicca was defeated, the rebuilding of Roman London started.

By AD 200 thick walls encircled the city, now the largest settlement in Britain. It consisted of an enormous forum – where Gracechurch Street now stands – with lawcourts, bathhouses, shops, meeting places, halls,

Must See

Roman remains

At the Guildhall Art Gallery (open to the public) you can see the remains of a Roman amphitheatre, discovered in the Guildhall Yard.
www.cityoflondon.gov.uk

and houses with fine mosaic floors and glass windows. But gradually the Romans' hold loosened and by AD 400 their rule was diminishing. A century later, Roman London was a shadow of its former glory.

Roman palace
A Roman governor's palace by the river had a pool, apartments, halls and offices – Cannon Street Station now covers the site.

By the year 600 Saxons had settled the area and gradually their 'Lundenwic' saw the revival of trade with ships using the river. But in 851 marauding Vikings sacked the city. However, in 886 the brilliant leadership of King Alfred of Wessex inspired the English to re-take the city. New streets were built, tradespeople and craftsmen welcomed, and new waterfronts established for commerce.

A London so commercially important continued to attract predatory Danish and Norwegian Vikings. By 1016, after decades of trying to buy off the attackers with danegeld (silver coin), England was under Danish rule, with King Cnut on the throne.

Saxon grip and pommel

When Cnut's son Harthacnut died in 1042, the throne came back to English rule. Pious Edward the Confessor was crowned and chose a site for his 'West Minster' and palace, and so Westminster became the centre for royal justice and administration. Edward died just after his great church was consecrated in 1065. His was the first burial there.

Must See

London Bridge

'London Bridge is falling down,' goes the old song and the crossing over the Thames between Southwark and the City has been replaced several times since that first Roman bridge. Between 1176 and 1209 the first stone structure was built across the river. A bridge built by

John Rennie in the late 1820s was taken apart and sold as a tourist attraction in Arizona, USA, when the present London Bridge was opened in 1973.
www.thelondonbridge experience.com

THE NORMANS

1066–1154

King William I, the Norman Conqueror, was the first sovereign to be crowned in Westminster Abbey, on Christmas Day 1066. As Duke of Normandy, he had invaded England, defeating the army of King Harold II at the Battle of Hastings in October that year.

William's rule made London a centre of a new Norman-French culture and language. It was the heart of Norman rule. William commissioned the Domesday Book, a unique record of land-holdings and wealth in the country. He oversaw the building of imposing castles, keeps, churches and

Must See

The Tower of London
The Romans chose the site of the Tower of London to build a wall and a defensive turret, and this was where William the Conqueror built what we now call the White Tower to defend his new capital and to impress his subjects. The massive tower was complete by 1100 although work continued over the centuries.

towers, including the White Tower, the massive fortress at the heart of the Tower of London. His son, William II, saw the completion of the Domesday Book after his father's death in 1087. He was responsible for Westminster Hall, built in 1097–99 and now part of the Houses of Parliament.

The Tower of London is one of the most impressive examples of military architecture in the world. It has served as a fortress and palace, prison and place of execution. The Royal Observatory, The Royal Mint, a menagerie and public records have all been housed here. The Crown

Jewels are kept here in tight security, as is a superb collection of royal arms and armour. The Tower covers 7ha (18 acres) and actually consists of 20 separate towers, set within concentric walls for security. It was Henry III who, in 1240, ordered the White Tower to be painted, giving rise to its name, and who turned it into a comfortable palace – although it was never the main royal residence. The Tudors saw the bloodiest use of the Tower, and in the 1500s executions on Tower Hill were commonplace. Now millions of visitors come each year to see the Crown Jewels, the armouries and the Tower itself with its 'Beefeaters' or Yeomen Warders, who wear a distinctive uniform that dates from Tudor days. *www.hrp.org.uk/TowerOfLondon*

Westminster Hall
This is the oldest surviving part of the Palace of Westminster, built in 1097 for William II who, reportedly, was not that impressed with it. But it is a wonderful hall with a magnificent hammerbeam roof added at the beginning of the 15th century, the largest unsupported timber structure in England. The hall was used as a court, seeing the state trials of William Wallace, Anne Boleyn, Charles I and Guy Fawkes. More recently it has been used at funerals for the lying-in-state of Sir Winston Churchill in 1965 and Queen Elizabeth the Queen Mother in 2002. *www.parliament.uk*

Must See

Survivor
St Bartholomew the Great, founded in Smithfield in 1123, was one of the few churches to survive the Great Fire of 1666 and has the most significant Norman interior of all London churches. www.greatsbarts.com

THE MIDDLE AGES

1154–1485

The Norman dynasty ended in 1154 with the death of King Stephen, who had spent much of his reign fighting his cousin Matilda for the Crown. The throne passed to Matilda's son, Henry II, who became the most powerful sovereign in Europe on his marriage to Eleanor of Aquitaine and the acquisition of land that accrued with the union.

Henry and his long Plantagenet line saw the establishment of the powerful trade guilds, based in the City of London, creating fine buildings, wealth, ceremony, and a structure for commerce and business.

OLD FISH STREET HILL EC4

Here shops opened to sell goods directly to passers-by, while market stalls filled the middle of the road. Side streets were named after the trades that operated in them. Threadneedle Street was the tailors' district, Bread Street contained bakeries, while fish was sold in Fish Street Hill.

Once again the biggest factor in the renewed prosperity was the River Thames. Barges brought grain, timber and stone up the river from other parts of Britain, while merchant ships carried imported goods such as wine and silk from overseas, and exported English wool and cloth to Europe and beyond.

Must See

The City of London

The famous 'square mile' that today comprises the City of London, with the Bank of England and the Stock Exchange at its heart, has its roots in medieval times, when the guilds – the trade associations supporting businesses as diverse as mercers (cloth merchants), grocers, goldsmiths, fishmongers, tailors and haberdashers – grew in power and status. The guilds controlled the wages and labour conditions of their members. The magnificent Guildhall, still at the centre of City life, was built in 1411 and, although partly damaged in the fire of 1666 and in the Blitz of 1940, survives in restored splendour. *www.cityoflondon.gov.uk*

Worshipful Companies

Today there are more than 100 livery companies in the City, although their purpose is now mainly charitable and ceremonial. These 'Worshipful Companies' still play a big part in the annual Lord Mayor's Show (pictured right) when their colourful and luxurious ceremonial garments are worn.

Must See

Leadenhall Market

In the heart of the City, this atmospheric market has been a place of commerce, and buying and selling for more than 800 years. The weekday market sells everything from fresh food and luxury goods to jewellery and paintings. Harry Potter fans will recognize it as Diagon Alley where Harry and his friends go to buy wands, gowns and books. *www.leadenhallmarket.co.uk*

London's river

The River Thames is, at 346km (215 miles), the longest river in England. It flows from Thames Head in Gloucestershire, through eight counties before reaching London – where it becomes tidal with a rise and fall of 7m (23ft). Its historical importance, in establishing the Port of London and the city itself, is huge. In a former sugar warehouse on West India Quay, Canary Wharf, is the Museum of London Docklands where you can discover the history of London as one of the greatest ports in the world.
www.museumindocklands.org.uk

THE MIDDLE AGES

1154–1485

While London prospered commercially in the Middle Ages, noblemen vied to take part in the crusades, battles to spread Christianity throughout the Middle East and Africa. It was during this time that the Knights Templar – crusading Christian warriors – grew in status and numbers. Many fine churches were built in London during the Middle Ages including the Temple Church, consecrated in 1185.

Perhaps the most significant building project was the rebuilding of Edward the Confessor's Westminster Abbey during the years 1220–72. Henry III, son of the notorious King John, was an admirer of Edward, naming his eldest son after the pious king. In the 1200s Henry ordered the new building, helping to carry the bones of the Confessor to their present burial place. He himself was interred there in 1272.

Eleanor Cross
Outside Charing Cross Station, to the south of Trafalgar Square, you will see a memorial to Queen Eleanor of Castile, who married the future Edward I of England in 1254. When she died in the north of England, Edward arranged for her funeral cortège to travel to London, ordering a great cross showing a likeness of his queen to be built at each stopping place on the route. The last, in marble, stood at Charing Cross, not far from Westminster Abbey where she was buried. The Eleanor Cross of today is an 1868 Victorian reproduction, the original having been destroyed.

Henry VII Chapel, Westminster Abbey

Temple Church

Tucked away between Fleet Street and the Thames is a quiet oasis of ancient buildings, including the beautiful and historic Temple Church. The church is constructed in two parts – the round church, which echoes the circular Church of the Holy Sepulchre in Jerusalem, and the chancel. Now the church is used by members of two Inns of Court, the Middle and Inner Temples. It is well known for the excellence of its music – and for the fact that it figures prominently in the popular novel and film *The Da Vinci Code*. www.templechurch.com

Must See

Westminster Abbey

Must See

A marshy swamp was the site chosen by King Edward the Confessor to build his 'West Minster' in 1065. The coronation of nearly every British monarch since William the Conqueror has taken place here. Henry III rebuilt the abbey 200 years later, ensuring that Edward's bones were laid to rest nearby. It was consecrated in 1269. Parts of the building are 11th century but the 13th and 14th centuries were when most of what we see today was built. Here you'll find Poets' Corner where many great British poets, including Blake, Shelley, Burns, Tennyson, Wordsworth and Byron, are remembered. It was not until the early 18th century that Westminster Abbey's distinctive west towers were built by architect Nicholas Hawksmoor. The Crown Jewels were kept here until 1303, when some went missing, and they were moved to the Tower of London. The House of Commons met in the abbey's Chapter House for more than 200 years. www.westminsterabbey.org

First edition
William Caxton set up the first printing press at Westminster in 1476. The first book to be printed here was Chaucer's The Canterbury Tales.

THE TUDORS

Henry Tudor, Earl of Richmond, supported the Lancastrian cause in the Wars of the Roses which had divided the country for 30 years. In 1485 he defeated King Richard III, who was killed at the Battle of Bosworth Field, and, as Henry VII, claimed the throne for the House of Tudor. Henry's rule brought stability to London, but it was his son, the larger-than-life Henry VIII, who oversaw the building of royal palaces, the foundation of naval dockyards in Greenwich and Deptford, ship-building, the enclosure of land for royal hunting parks and the dissolution of the monasteries. Elizabeth I, born in 1533, daughter of Henry VIII and Anne Boleyn, ruled over a London which saw the development of exploration, the theatre, poetry, literature, painting and the arts.

St James's Palace

Tudor rose
The warring Yorkists, whose symbol was a white rose, and Lancastrians (a red rose) were united when Henry VII married Elizabeth of York after the Battle of Bosworth Field. The red and white Tudor rose was a powerful symbol of this new unity.

Horse Guards

Between Horse Guards Road and Whitehall is an archway guarded by two mounted troopers of The Household Cavalry. This is Horse Guards, built on the yard where Henry VIII and his soldiers used to joust. The archway leads to Horse Guards Parade, where HM the Queen takes the salute at Trooping the Colour each year. There is a colourful Changing the Guard here daily.
www.changing-the-guard.com

Must See

Henry VIII seized York Place, the home of the disgraced Cardinal Wolsey, for his Palace of Whitehall. He also commandeered a leper hospital dedicated to St James, which was rebuilt as St James's Palace and whose original brick gatehouse survives. This is the oldest royal palace, full of historical significance and still considered home to the royal court. Mary I died here and her half-sister Elizabeth I is thought to have slept here while waiting for the Spanish Armada to strike. Charles I spent his last night at St James's before his execution. His son Charles II used it as a base to visit his mistress Nell Gwyn in nearby Pall Mall. A number of British monarchs, including Queen Victoria, have been married here. Today it is home to several members of the Royal Family, while Prince William and Prince Harry have the offices of their household here. The palace is not open to the public.

Palace of Whitehall
Henry VIII's great Palace of Whitehall, the main location of the royal court, once covered 9ha (23 acres). There were tennis courts, an orchard, steps leading to the river, a tiltyard for jousting tournaments, a cockfighting pit, royal apartments, a chapel and a great hall. Here the king married Anne Boleyn in 1533, then Jane Seymour three years later, and here he died.

Shakespeare's Globe

Must See

In 1599, when William Shakespeare belonged to acting company The Lord Chamberlain's Men, the Globe Theatre was built by the Thames at Southwark. Thirteen years later it burnt down when a cannon misfired during a performance of *Henry VIII*. The Globe was soon rebuilt, but eventually closed by the Puritans in the early 1640s. The Shakespeare Globe Trust faithfully recreated a new Globe, which opened in 1997.
www.shakespearesglobe.org

THE STUARTS

1603–1714

James Stuart, son of Mary Queen of Scots, was already King James VI of Scotland when Elizabeth I died in 1603. As her heir, he became James I, England's first Stuart monarch. He survived the Gunpowder Plot in 1605, but his son Charles I was beheaded in 1649 after the country had been torn apart by several years of civil war between Charles' Royalist forces and the Parliamentarians, led by Oliver Cromwell. Eleven years of Puritan rule under Cromwell's Protectorate followed before the restoration of the monarchy, when Charles II returned from exile to be crowned in 1660.

The Great Fire of London, the worst of several conflagrations in London, raged for four days in 1666, destroying more than three-quarters of the buildings in the City. A rebuilding programme followed when Sir Christopher Wren's St Paul's Cathedral arose from the ashes, along with many other beautiful churches.

Remember, remember
Roman Catholic dissidents plotted to blow up the Palace of Westminster, intending to kill the Protestant King James I during the Opening of Parliament on 5 November 1605. An intercepted letter gave the game away and a search revealed explosives and Guy Fawkes, one of the plotters, hiding in a vault beneath the palace.

John Donne
A memorial to metaphysical poet and Dean of St Paul's, John Donne (1573–1631), is one of hundreds to be found in St Paul's Cathedral. It is unique in that it is the only statue of any significance to have survived the fire that destroyed the old cathedral in 1666.

Must See

St Paul's Cathedral

Ludgate Hill, crowned with Wren's magnificent St Paul's Cathedral, is where the inhabitants of London have chosen to build their places of worship for centuries. There is evidence that the Romans may have constructed a temple on this high ground. The first Christian church in London, dedicated to St Paul, was built here by Ethelbert, King of Kent. St Paul, who was martyred by the sword in Rome, has been London's patron saint ever since. That first church on the site was a wooden structure and three more were built before the present St Paul's was designed. Christopher Wren had been asked to submit designs to replace the enormous 'old' St Paul's before the Great Fire burned it to the ground in 1666. Wren, who rebuilt much of the city (more than 13,000 houses and nearly 90 churches were destroyed in the fire), completed the enormous domed cathedral on his 76th birthday in 1708. After his death, Wren was honoured by burial in his cathedral – as many great men and women have been over the centuries. His epitaph is simple: in translation it reads, 'If you seek his monument, look around you'. St Paul's contains many memorials to national figures. It is also traditionally a place for important national ceremonies. *www.stpauls.co.uk*

THE STUARTS

A short journey down river is Greenwich. In Tudor times the Royal
Palace of Placentia was the favourite home of Henry VII, and the
birthplace of both Henry VIII and Elizabeth I. But it was the Stuarts who
developed the Greenwich we see today, a World Heritage Site full of
historical interest.

Must See

The Royal Observatory
Charles II set up his Royal Observatory in Greenwich to
discover how to measure longitude and so improve navigation. In 1884 the
Greenwich Meridian became internationally recognized as Longitude 0° – the
centre of world time and the starting point of each day, year and millennium.
www.nmm.ac.uk

The Old Royal Naval College

This was designed as a hospital by
Sir Christopher Wren and Nicholas Hawksmoor
on the site of the Palace of Placentia, which
was pulled down after the Civil War. The
stunning Painted Hall (see right), Queen Mary
Chapel, Visitor Centre, permanent exhibition
Discover Greenwich, opened in 2010, and
grounds are open daily, free of charge.
www.oldroyalnavalcollege.org

National Maritime Museum
This museum incorporates the Royal Observatory, the Time and Space
Project – an astronomy centre with a 120-seat planetarium – and the 17th-
century Queen's House. Set in the magnificent 80-ha (200-acre) Greenwich
Royal Park, the museum has more than two million exhibits, including maps,
maritime art, models, manuscripts and navigational instruments, reflecting the
great seafaring history of the British Isles. *www.nmm.ac.uk*

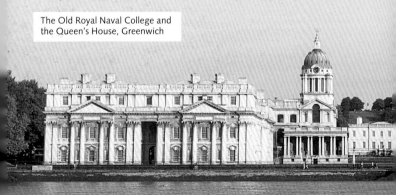

The Old Royal Naval College and
the Queen's House, Greenwich

In the 17th century the Covent Garden area west of the City was developed by architect Inigo Jones for its owner the Duke of Bedford. The great piazza soon became a focus for street traders and entertainers. The Royal Opera House (see left) was built in 1732 but extensively remodelled at the end of the 20th century, making it one of the most modern theatres in Europe. *www.roh.org.uk*

Must See

Covent Garden

In the Middle Ages a large fruit and vegetable garden, worked by the monks of St Peter's Abbey, flourished here. The 'Convent Garden' supplied fresh produce to much of London, but at the Reformation in the 16th century the land went to the Dukes of Bedford. In the early 17th century Inigo Jones' new design had a great arcaded square at its heart with the church of St Paul's fronting one side. Soon street traders set up, selling exotic food and imported goods. Entertainers appeared – diarist

Samuel Pepys records seeing a Punch and Judy show in 1662. After the Great Fire of 1666, Covent Garden became the most important market in the city, until the 20th century saw it specialize in wholesale fruit and vegetables. In 1974 the wholesale business was moved, but by 1980 Covent Garden was redeveloped as a tourist and shopping area, and has become famous for its street theatre.

London Transport Museum

At this absorbing museum in Covent Garden, displays of vehicles, from trams and trolleybuses to a steam locomotive from the old Metropolitan Railway (which became the London Underground), can be seen. *www.ltmuseum.co.uk*

England expects …
The body of Admiral Lord Nelson was brought to lie in state in the Painted Hall after his death at the Battle of Trafalgar in 1805. He was buried in St Paul's where his tomb can be visited.

Round the world
In 1967 Sir Francis Chichester was knighted on the steps of the Old Royal Naval College by HM the Queen for his solo circumnavigation of the world in his yacht Gypsy Moth IV.

THE STUARTS

The bright lights of Piccadilly Circus may look completely 21st century, but this area of London was developed in Stuart times, as was exclusive Mayfair. The Banqueting House in Whitehall and Kensington Palace, home over the years to many members of the Royal Family, were built then too.

Piccadill
Piccadilly was so-called in the 17th century in honour of a 'piccadill', a fashionable lace-frilled collar. Before that, it was called Portugal Street.

Piccadilly Circus

Piccadilly

Must See

After the restoration of the monarchy in 1660, when Charles II was crowned king, Piccadilly – one of the broadest streets in London – became a fashionable address. Now luxury hotels, including The Ritz (left), shops such as Fortnum & Mason and Hatchards, and some expensive apartments, line the street.

The West End is the beating heart of London's nightlife, with theatres, night clubs, cinemas and music venues. At its hub is neon-lit Piccadilly Circus where five streets converge. From here you can shop in Regent Street or take tea at The Ritz on Piccadilly. Shaftesbury Avenue and the Haymarket are at the centre of theatreland. Her Majesty's Theatre (1897), which specializes in major musical productions, and the Theatre Royal (1820) are both in Haymarket. Shaftesbury Avenue theatres include the Lyric of 1888; the Apollo, Gielgud and Queen's (pictured) all opened in the early 1900s.

May Fair
Mayfair is one of the most expensive addresses in the world, with exclusive shopping and some of the most luxurious hotels in London. Ironically, it was named for the rowdy 'May Fair' that took place here annually, until it was moved in the late 18th century because it lowered the tone of the neighbourhood.

Hay market
In the 16th and 17th centuries, Haymarket – a broad street linking Pall Mall and Piccadilly – was a market for selling cattle fodder.

Must See

Kensington Palace
William III of Orange bought Nottingham House in 1689 because he wanted country air to help his asthma. Kensington was a village then, and architects Sir Christopher Wren and Nicholas Hawksmoor converted the country house into something much grander – Kensington Palace (pictured left). Victoria was born here and here she was told she was queen. The palace was home to Prince Charles, Princess Diana, Prince William and Prince Harry, and still today several members of the Royal Family live here. Kensington Palace is open to the public. *www.hrp.org.uk*

Banqueting House
This unique building is all that remains of the original Palace of Whitehall which was destroyed by fire in 1698. Inigo Jones' Banqueting House is classical Italian Renaissance in style. It is built on three floors with a double height banqueting hall which has a ceiling painted by Sir Peter Paul Rubens. *www.hrp.org.uk*

THE GEORGIANS

1714–1837

When George I became king in 1714, he spoke German, not English, so Britain's first Prime Minister, Robert Walpole, saw to affairs of government. Walpole took up residence in Downing Street where Prime Ministers have lived ever since. The Napoleonic Wars, a series of conflicts with the French, were towards the end of the Georgian era; Trafalgar Square was planned to celebrate Nelson's naval victory in 1805. The square's architect John Nash also planned grand streets and terraces, examples of which may be seen around Regent's Park.

Must See

Trafalgar Square
Tourists flock to this square, with its towering column topped by the statue of Admiral Lord Nelson. Part of this space was occupied for 300 years by the Great Mews, the royal stables. The area was cleared by architect John Nash and in 1830 named Trafalgar Square. Nelson's Column has, at its base, four enormous bronze lions by Sir Edwin Landseer. The impressive fountains were designed by Sir Edwin Lutyens in 1935. Trafalgar Square is a focus for national celebration and political protest.
www.london.gov.uk/trafalgarsquare

Regent's Park, planned by the Prince Regent and Nash, was first opened to the public in 1845. Today there are gardens, an open air theatre (pictured below), a boating lake, sports facilities and playgrounds. Here too is London Zoo, the world's oldest scientific zoo, which was the first in the world to open a reptile house, a children's zoo, a public aquarium and an insect house. *www.royalparks.org.uk, www.zsl.org*

Pooh Bear
When writer A.A. Milne visited London Zoo with his son, Christopher Robin, the young boy fell in love with Winnipeg (Winnie) Bear, an American black bear. And so Winnie-the-Pooh, star of one of the best-loved children's books ever, was born.

Must See

Regent Street
Regent Street, known for its shops and fantastic Christmas decorations, was named for the Prince Regent who, by the time the street was completed in 1825, was King George IV.

Number Ten
Number 10 Downing Street is one of the world's most famous addresses. The official residence of the British Prime Minister, with its black door in a stone surround and a large '10' under the fanlight, is a familiar image. The Chancellor of the Exchequer lives next door, at number 11.

Must See

The Royal Academy
Run by distinguished artists and architects, this is in Burlington House, Piccadilly, where exhibitions – including the famous Summer Exhibition – are mounted. *www.royalacademy.org.uk*

The Royal Mews
The horses and coaches used on royal ceremonial occasions are kept at these mews near Buckingham Palace. Built by John Nash, they house 30 horses (Cleveland Bays and Windsor Greys) in gleaming stables, and magnificent coaches, including the fairy-tale Gold State Coach. The Royal Mews are open during the summer and early autumn. *www.royalcollection.org.uk*

St Martin-in-the-Fields
This famous church stands on the east side of Trafalgar Square. Designed by James Gibbs in 1721, it is well-known for its help with the homeless, its concerts and its popular café in the crypt. It is the parish church of the Royal Family. *www.stmartin-in-the-fields.org*

THE VICTORIANS

Although William IV had ten children, none was legitimate, so his niece Victoria, the daughter of his late brother the Duke of Kent, became queen at the age of 18. Victoria reigned for 64 years. She married her beloved Prince Albert in 1840, the marriage proving a partnership that saw London enriched by the Great Exhibition of 1851, which funded the Natural History Museum, the Victoria and Albert Museum and the Science Museum. The National Gallery and National Portrait Gallery also opened during her reign.

The National Gallery

Opened in 1838, this is one of the great art collections of the world, with works from the mid-13th century to 1900, representing most major movements in Western European art. Nearby, in St Martin's Place, is the National Portrait Gallery which houses paintings and sculpture of historically important and famous Britons. Its first exhibit was the 'Chandos' painting said to be of William Shakespeare.
www.nationalgallery.org.uk,
www.npg.org.uk

Kensington

Kensington High Street (pictured below) is where the locals shop but South Kensington is the place if you are interested in natural history, science or the arts. This is museum-land, the so-called 'Albertopolis', funded partly with money raised from the Great Exhibition of 1851 in which Prince Albert was a prime mover.

Victoria and Albert Museum

The world's largest museum of art and design, the V&A houses collections of decorative and artistic material including ceramics, glass, prints, textiles, silver, costume, jewellery, sculpture, and Asian and Islamic art. *www.vam.ac.uk*

Natural History Museum

The high-roofed exhibition halls of this wonderful museum (pictured right) are a favourite with children clamouring to see the enormous dinosaur skeletons. Five main collections (plants, insects, prehistory, minerals and zoology) contain an amazing 70 million exhibits. One of the most popular exhibits includes the skeleton of Dippy the dinosaur (*Diplodocus carnegeii*). *www.nhm.ac.uk*

The National Gallery

Science Museum

Here you can explore space and see the earliest steam engines, including Stephenson's *Rocket* and *Puffing Billy*, and the first jet engine. You can learn about the structure of DNA and explore medical history, see the evidence for climate change and bring science alive with interactive exhibits. *www.sciencemuseum.org.uk*

Albert Memorial

When Prince Albert, Queen Victoria's much-loved consort, died in 1861 at the age of 42, a memorial that took more than 10 years to complete was designed by Sir George Gilbert Scott. You can see this high-Victorian extravaganza in Kensington Gardens. Albert, covered in gold leaf, sits under a canopy surrounded by sculpted groups representing Europe, Africa, Asia and America, and depictions celebrating manufacturing, farming, engineering and the arts.

Royal Albert Hall

Nearby the Royal Albert Hall also pays tribute to Albert's memory. Built as The Central Hall of Arts and Sciences, the hall was renamed by the bereaved queen as she laid the foundation stone. Opened in 1871, the Albert Hall has hosted major artists from around the world. It has been home to the world's largest music festival, the annual summer Proms concerts, since 1941. *www.royalalberthall.com*

THE VICTORIANS

Just before Victoria became queen, the Houses of Parliament burned down and their replacement was commissioned. During her reign, Joseph Paxton's Crystal Palace housed the Great Exhibition, the first international and industrial show of its kind, attracting visitors from all corners of the globe. Tower Bridge, so-called because of its proximity to the ancient Tower of London, was designed by Sir John Wolfe Barry to provide a new crossing of the River Thames, and to allow shipping to pass safely into the Pool of London. It was opened in 1894.

The Houses of Parliament

'Mind the gap'
In 1863 London's underground railway – commonly called 'the tube' – opened. The famous Underground map, designed by Harry Beck in 1933, shows the locations of the stations with the lines drawn in different colours, and is regarded as a design classic, as is the 'roundel' announcing the name of each station.

Chelsea sets
The Victorian climate allowed 19th-century artists and writers such as Rossetti, Turner, Holman Hunt, Whistler, Swinburne and Carlyle to flourish, forming an artists' colony in Chelsea. A century later, in the 'Swinging Sixties', King's Road, Chelsea, was the place to be. The Beatles, Eric Clapton and The Rolling Stones all lived here, while Vivienne Westwood and her then husband Malcolm McLaren, manager of punk band The Sex Pistols, opened a shop selling punk gear.

Houses of Parliament

The Palace of Westminster contains the House of Commons, the House of Lords and Westminster Hall. The medieval hall was the only part not destroyed in the fire of 1834. The new building was the work of architects Charles Barry, the classicist, and Augustus Pugin, whose taste was Gothic. Between them they designed a great building, classical in concept but Gothic in decoration. Outside is a statue of Oliver Cromwell who, in the 17th century, ensured the supremacy of Parliament over the monarchy. The 98-m (320-ft) clock tower that houses Big Ben, the bell with the famous chimes, towers above the palace. *www.parliament.uk*

Hyde Park

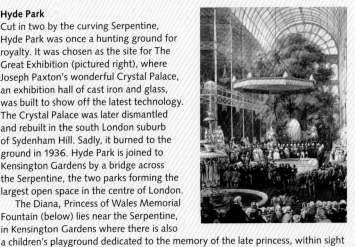

Cut in two by the curving Serpentine, Hyde Park was once a hunting ground for royalty. It was chosen as the site for The Great Exhibition (pictured right), where Joseph Paxton's wonderful Crystal Palace, an exhibition hall of cast iron and glass, was built to show off the latest technology. The Crystal Palace was later dismantled and rebuilt in the south London suburb of Sydenham Hill. Sadly, it burned to the ground in 1936. Hyde Park is joined to Kensington Gardens by a bridge across the Serpentine, the two parks forming the largest open space in the centre of London.

The Diana, Princess of Wales Memorial Fountain (below) lies near the Serpentine, in Kensington Gardens where there is also a children's playground dedicated to the memory of the late princess, within sight

of her former apartments at Kensington Palace. An 11-km (7-mile) memorial walk follows a route through four of the Royal Parks – Kensington Gardens, Hyde Park, Green Park and St James's Park. Hyde Park, where protestors congregate, rock concerts are held and free speech is maintained at Speakers' Corner, is open to all. *www.royalparks.org.uk*

Tower Bridge

Tower Bridge, with its mock-Gothic towers, was built in 1886–94 when a new crossing of the River Thames was needed. The bridge had to allow shipping to pass safely through into the Pool of London, so a bascule bridge was designed – with two arms that were raised hydraulically. Today's visitors may enjoy the views from the high walkways and admire the magnificent Victorian engineering room. *www.towerbridge.org.uk*

Must See

Westminster Cathedral
The country's leading Roman
Catholic church, Westminster Cathedral in
Francis Street, Victoria, has an extraordinary
façade that owes much to the early Christian
Byzantine style. Towers, domes and balconies
decorate the front of this red brick and white
Portland stone building, where worship started
in 1903. Inside, much of the decoration,
including mosaics, sculpture, kneelers and
inlaid ebony, was made by members of the
Arts and Crafts Movement. The 14 stations
of the cross were carved by sculptor Eric Gill.
www.westminstercathedral.org.uk

The early years of the 20th century saw both the completion of the Roman Catholic Westminster Cathedral and the opening of flagship store Selfridges in Oxford Street. Bloomsbury, already the home of the British Museum, became known for the intellectuals who flourished there, before and after the First World War that changed so many lives for ever. George V, the first monarch of the House of Windsor, became king in 1910 after his elder brother died, while his son George VI was crowned after the abdication of his brother Edward VII in 1936. Thus a death and an abdication changed the line of succession, so that it was HM Queen Elizabeth II who acceded to the throne in 1952.

Bloomsbury

Along Shaftesbury Avenue and Gower Street is Bloomsbury, home to the British Museum and the Royal Academy of Dramatic Arts (RADA). Bloomsbury is perhaps best known for the writers and artists who lived here in the early 20th century working in a spirit of rebellion against what they saw as the conventional lifestyle of the previous generation.

British Museum

In Bloomsbury is one of the world's great museums, representing culture, ancient and modern, drawn from across the nations. The museum was first opened in 1759, but it was in the 20th century that it underwent a great expansion. With its famous colonnaded portico, the British Museum is London's top visitor attraction, holding around seven million objects in the collections. They include the sculptures of the Parthenon Frieze (see below), the Rosetta Stone, which allowed Egyptologists to decipher hieroglyphics, and the Portland Vase – a violet-blue Roman cameo vase. The British Library was once part of the museum but is now housed in Euston Road, next to St Pancras Station.
www.britishmuseum.org

Broadcasting House

The iconic art deco headquarters of the BBC was opened in 1932 in Portland Place, which is at the northern end of Regent Street. At the front of the building are Eric Gill's sculptures of Prospero and Ariel from Shakespeare's *The Tempest*. Prospero, the magician, and Ariel, a creature of the air, were chosen to represent the spirit of the BBC. Next door in Langham Place is All Souls Church with its circular portico and stone spire, consecrated in 1824.

THE HOUSE OF WINDSOR

1910–present

In 1940–41 the Blitz started in London with 57 consecutive nights of bombing, causing extensive damage and loss of life. Its aim was to demoralize the people of London; but this failed as civilians and uniformed organizations rallied together to rise to the challenge and 'do their bit'. After the destruction, the coronation of Queen Elizabeth II in Westminster Abbey came as a breath of fresh air. The weary nation watched with enthusiasm as the Queen and Prince Philip moved into Buckingham Palace with their young family.

The 'Swinging Sixties' brought a new youth culture to areas such as Carnaby Street and Soho. The post-war rebuilding of London included the South Bank, the Barbican, Canary Wharf and the Docklands. The London Millennium Footbridge and the London Eye celebrated the new millennium, while the year 2012 sees London welcome Olympic athletes.

Must See

Soho

Soho has always had a Bohemian reputation. Until the late 20th century it was known mostly for its strip clubs, night life, music, lively pubs and film industry. 'Hippies' and 'mods' flocked to Carnaby Street to buy clothes in the sixties, and listen to music in the underground bars and in the legendary Marquee Club in Wardour Street. Now some of the sleaze has been swept away with the influx of fashionable restaurants and upmarket offices. One of the world's great jazz clubs, Ronnie Scott's, is now in Frith Street. Chinese stone lions and elaborate gates tell you that you are entering Chinatown (right) in the area around Gerrard Street, where there are street festivals, Chinese restaurants and shops selling authentic Chinese goods.

www.carnaby.co.uk, www.ronniescotts.co.uk

Buckingham Palace

HM the Queen lives in the north wing of Buckingham Palace and the Royal Standard flutters overhead when she is in residence. Queen Victoria was the first sovereign to make the palace the official royal home. The ornate State Apartments, used for ceremonial occasions, are open to the public every summer. The Queen's Gallery, where you can see works of art from the Royal Collection, is open daily. *www.royal.gov.uk*

Must See

Clarence House

Clarence House, next to St James's Palace, is open for a few weeks each summer. For nearly 50 years this elegant four-storied stucco house was home to the Queen Mother. Now Prince Charles, his wife the Duchess of Cornwall, and sons Prince William and Prince Harry, live here. www.royal.gov.uk

London, an exciting multicultural city, has one of the most ethnically diverse populations in the world, with more than 300 different languages spoken by inhabitants from Asian, African, Chinese, Greek and many other non-British groups. This vibrant capital, trading centre and port has always attracted overseas visitors and residents eager to enjoy one of the great cities of the world.

AD 43 Claudius leads Roman invasion and settles troops in Londinium.

c. 50 First London Bridge built.

60–61 The Iceni, led by Boudicca, rout the Romans and burn the city.

62–200 Roman Londinium rebuilt and the port established.

c. 200 City walls built.

400–500 Roman rule diminishes.

604 First St Paul's Cathedral built.

c. 600–800 Saxons develop Lundenwic; skirmishes with invading Vikings.

886 Alfred the Great vanquishes Vikings.

1065 First Westminster Abbey consecrated; Edward the Confessor is buried there.

1066 William of Normandy crowned in Westminster Abbey.

1078 Tower of London's White Tower begun.

1097 William II (Rufus) orders building of Westminster Hall.

1123 St Bartholomew the Great in Smithfield, one of London's oldest churches, founded.

1154 The Plantagenet line starts with coronation of Henry II.

1185 Temple Church consecrated.

1269 Consecration of rebuilt Westminster Abbey.

1303 Crown Jewels moved to Tower of London for safekeeping.

1415 Henry V celebrates victory over French at Agincourt with triumphal procession.

1476 William Caxton sets up first printing press near Westminster Abbey.

1491 Henry VIII born at Greenwich.

1532–36 Henry VIII builds St James's Palace and Whitehall Palace.

1536 Anne Boleyn executed at the Tower of London.

1599 Globe Theatre built at Southwark.

1605 Gunpowder Plot – Guy Fawkes captured and later tried and executed.

1649 Charles I executed in Whitehall; Commonwealth of England under Oliver Cromwell is declared.